Greedy Toad

'Greedy Toad'
An original concept by Tracy Gunaratnam
© Tracy Gunaratnam 2025

Illustrated by Angelika Scudamore

Published by MAVERICK ARTS PUBLISHING LTD
Suite 1, Hillreed House, 54 Queen Street,
Horsham, West Sussex, RH13 5AD
© Maverick Arts Publishing Limited April 2025
+44 (0)1403 256941

A CIP catalogue record for this book is available at the British Library.

ISBN 978-1-83511-055-3

Printed in India

www.maverickbooks.co.uk

This book is rated as: Turquoise Band (Guided Reading)

Greedy Toad

By Tracy Gunaratnam

Illustrated by Angelika Scudamore

One day, Greedy Toad caught Lucky Cricket on his long, sticky tongue.

"Yummy!" he croaked.

"A feast for the eyes, a treat for the nose, open wide and down she goes!"

"Excuse me!" said Lucky Cricket. "I'm not going anywhere without a crumpet. You can't eat crickets without crumpets. Everyone knows that."

"Hmm," Greedy Toad paused. "Crumpets are tasty. And I know just where to find one."

Greedy Toad tiptoed into Scary Bear's lair. And right there on Scary Bear's kitchen table, sat a large plate of crumpets.

Greedy Toad quickly snatched a crumpet from Scary Bear's plate, and off he hopped.

"A cricket and a crumpet! Yummy!" croaked Greedy Toad.

"A feast for the eyes, a treat for the nose, open wide and down she goes!"

"I don't think so!" said Lucky Cricket. "I'm not budging without lettuce. Everyone knows you can't eat crickets and crumpets without some crispy lettuce."

"Hmm," Greedy Toad paused. He liked crispy lettuce, and he knew just where to find some.

Greedy Toad crept into Scary Bear's garden.

Scary Bear's garden was beautiful.

He was growing lots of fruit and vegetables.

Greedy Toad saw the lettuces at the far side of the garden.

He hopped over as quietly as he could. Then he quickly snatched a fresh lettuce leaf from right between Scary Bear's huge, hairy feet. And off he hopped.

"A cricket, a crumpet and lettuce! Yummy!" croaked Greedy Toad.

"A feast for the eyes, a treat for the nose, open wide and down she goes!"

"Hold on!" said Lucky Cricket. "You've forgotten the most important ingredient of all!"

Greedy Toad's tummy was rumbling.

"What's that?" he asked.

"It's obvious," replied Lucky Cricket. You can't eat a cricket, a crumpet, and crispy lettuce without a ripe tomato."

"Why didn't I think of that?" croaked Greedy Toad. "Tomatoes are delicious. And I know just where to find one."

Greedy Toad hopped into Scary Bear's greenhouse. Scary Bear's greenhouse was the perfect spot for growing tomatoes; it always got lots of sunshine. Scary Bear was watering the tomatoes, so Greedy Toad waited as patiently as he could.

As soon as Scary Bear's huge, hairy back was turned, Greedy Toad jumped into action. He plucked a plump, juicy tomato from Scary Bear's tomato plant and off he hopped.

Greedy Toad couldn't wait to eat his towering snack. But unfortunately, he wasn't the only one.

Suddenly, without warning, a huge, hairy paw picked up Greedy Toad and his tall, tasty tower.

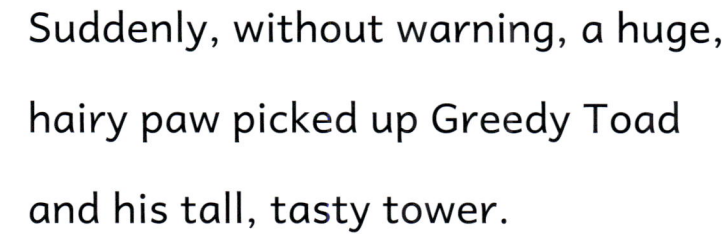

"**Yummy!**" growled Scary Bear. "I love crumpets with crispy lettuce, ripe tomato, and a greedy toad. But hang on, what's this?"

"A cricket! Yuck! I don't like crickets! Off you go!" he said. And he flicked Lucky Cricket into the long, green grass.

"Phew, that was lucky," said Lucky Cricket.

Scary Bear's tummy began to growl.

He opened his mouth wide and...

"Wait!" shouted Greedy Toad.

"What about the cheese? Everyone knows you can't eat a greedy toad, a crumpet, crispy lettuce and a ripe tomato without a big chunk of cheese!"

"Bears don't eat cheese," replied Scary Bear.

Scary bear held Greedy Toad and the tall, tasty tower right under his huge, hairy nose. He took a giant sniff, licked his lips and said, "A feast for the eyes, a treat for the nose, open wide and…"

Greedy Toad leapt out of the tasty tower and hopped away as fast as he could.

"Come back!" shouted Scary Bear as he chased after the toad. "Everyone knows you can't eat a crumpet, crispy lettuce and a ripe tomato without a big Greedy Toad!"

Lucky Cricket waved a four-leaf clover. "That'll teach Greedy Toad!" she said, and she bounced away to enjoy the day.

Quiz

1. How did Greedy Toad catch Lucky Cricket?
a) With a clever trap
b) On his long, sticky tongue
c) With his big, webbed hands

2. Where does Greedy Toad find a crumpet?
a) In Scary Bear's garden
b) On Scary Bear's plate
c) In Scary Bear's cupboard

3. "…you can't eat crickets and crumpets without some crispy _____."
a) crackers
b) tomato
c) lettuce

4. Who frees Lucky Cricket?
a) Greedy Toad
b) Lucky Cricket
c) Scary Bear

5. "Bears don't eat _____."
a) toads
b) crumpets
c) cheese

Book Bands for Guided Reading

The Institute of Education book banding system is a scale of colours that reflects the various levels of reading difficulty. The bands are assigned by taking into account the content, the language style, the layout and phonics. Word, phrase and sentence level work is also taken into consideration.

Maverick Early Readers are a bright, attractive range of books covering the pink to white bands. All of these books have been book banded for guided reading to the industry standard and edited by a leading educational consultant.

To view the whole Maverick Readers scheme, visit our website at www.maverickearlyreaders.com

Or scan the QR code above to view our scheme instantly!

Quiz Answers: 1b, 2b, 3c, 4c, 5c